BRAIN FITNESS BOOT CAMP

──── ROOKIE ────
BASIC TRAINING

THIS IS A CARLTON BOOK

Published by Carlton Books Limited
20 Mortimer Street
London W1T 3JW

ISBN 978 1 84732 935 6

The puzzles in this book were previously published in *Brain Training Puzzles Quick Book 1.*

Printed in China

──ROOKIE──
BASIC TRAINING

CARLTON

Introduction

Welcome to *Brain Fitness Boot Camp*, recruit!

Let me tell you something – brain fitness is just like physical fitness: if you don't use it, you are almost guaranteed to lose it!

So, if you'd rather not get your brain into shape, just put down this book and go watch some mind-numbing television until bedtime…

Still here? Good! You've signed up to *Brain Fitness Boot Camp* because you want your brain to be a lean, mean thinking machine – not a useless lump of grey sponge. Congratulations, recruit – you've proven that you're smarter than average already!

The puzzles in this book will give your brain a refreshing warm up and before long you'll be ready for even bigger challenges. We've got puzzles to test your observation, logic, basic numeracy and lateral thinking – all the ammunition you need to tackle life's mental obstacle course.

Always remember that your brain is one of the most amazing things you'll ever possess, so look after it. As well as keeping it busy, you should try to get enough sleep, eat a balanced diet and keep your stress levels down – and there's no better antidote to stress than having some fun. Yet another good reason for using this book.

So, have fun. That's an order!

Sergeant O'Brain. Drill Instructor.
Brain Fitness Boot Camp.

Bits and Pieces

How can you mend a broken heart? Here's four you can practise on. Match each half heart with its partner to make four whole ones.

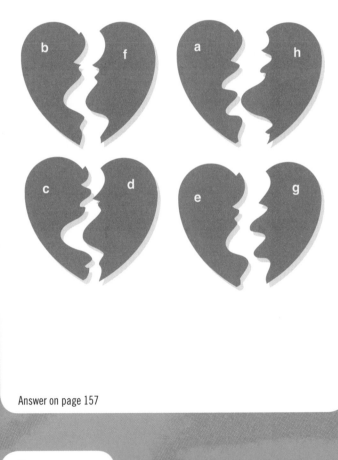

Answer on page 157

Boxes

Playing the game of boxes, each player takes it in turns to join two adjacent dots with a line. If a player's line completes a box, the player wins the box and has another go. It's your turn in the game below. To avoid giving your opponent a lot of boxes, what's your best move?

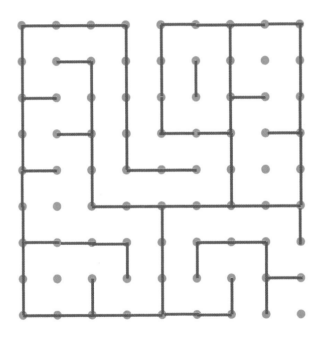

Answer on page 157

Colour Maze

Cross the maze from top to bottom. You may only pass from a green square to a red one, a red to a yellow, a yellow to a blue or a blue to a green, and you may not travel diagonally.

Answer on page 157

Cut and Fold

Which of the patterns below is created by this fold and cut?

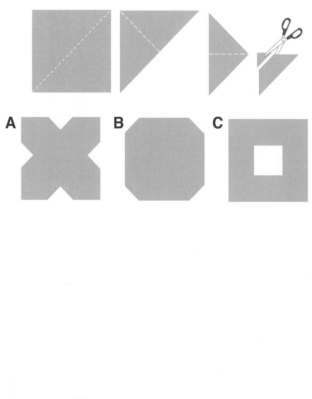

A

B

C

Answer on page 157

Double Drat

All these shapes appear twice in the box except one. Can you spot the singleton?

Answer on page 157

Game of Two Halves

Which two shapes below will pair up to create the top shape?

A 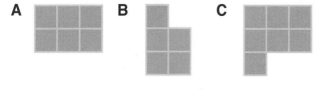 **B** **C**

D 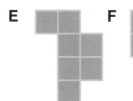 **E** **F**

Answer on page 157

Get the Picture

These two grids, when merged together, wil make a picture...
Of what?

Answer on page 157

Gridlock

Which square correctly completes the grid?

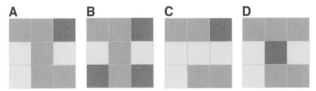

A **B** **C** **D**

Answer on page 157

In the Area

100 mm

Can you work out the approximate area that this dog is taking up?

Answer on page 158

Jigsaw

Which three of the pieces below can complete the jigsaw and make a perfect square?

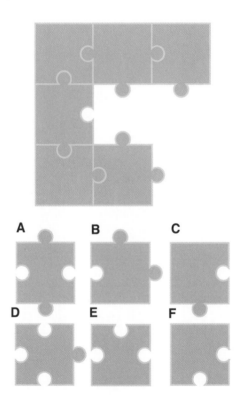

A

B

C

D

E

F

Answer on page 158

Where's the Pair?

Only two of these pictures are exactly the same. Can you spot the matching pair?

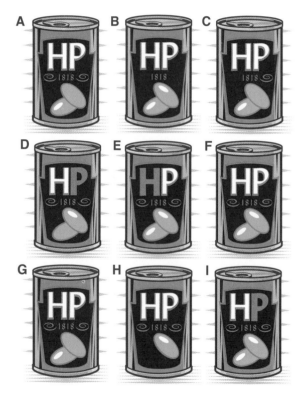

Answer on page 158

Symmetry

This picture, when finished, is symmetrical along a vertical line up the middle. Can you colour in the missing squares and work out what the picture is of?

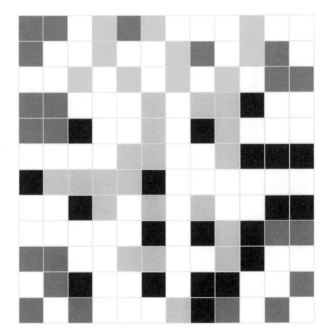

Answer on page 158

Sum People

Work out what number is represented by which person and replace the question mark.

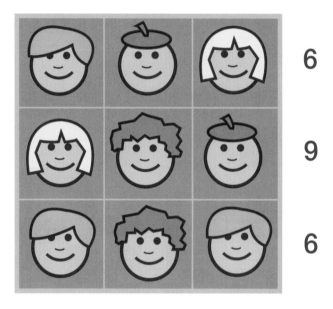

4   11   ?

Answer on page 158

Spot the Difference

Can you spot ten differences between this pair of pictures?

Answer on page 158

Shape Shifting

Fill in the empty squares so that each row, column and long diagonal contains five different symbols

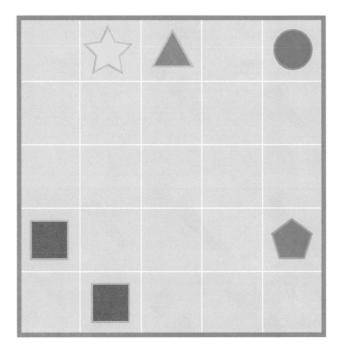

Answer on page 158

Scene It?

The four squares below can all be found in the picture grid – can you track them down? Beware, they may not be the right way up!

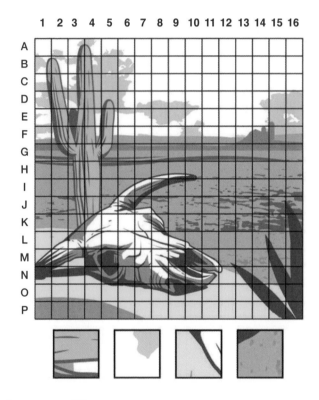

Answer on page 158

Rainbow Reckoning

This map can only be coloured in with three colours – blue, yellow and green. Assuming no two adjacent areas can be coloured the same, what colour will the area containing the question mark be?

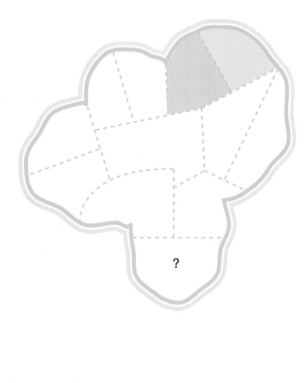

Answer on page 159

Pots of Dots

How many dots should there be in the hole in this pattern?

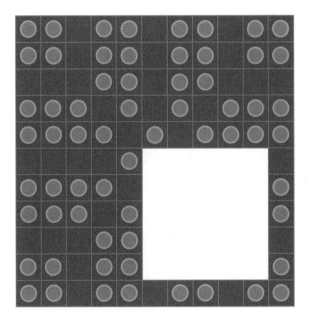

Answer on page 159

Picture Parts

Which box has exactly the right bits to make the pic?

Answer on page 159

Odd Clocks

Buenos Aires is 11 hours behind Singapore, which is 7 hours ahead of London. It is 6.55 pm on Tuesday in London – what time is it in the other two cities?

LONDON

SINGAPORE

BUENOS AIRES

Answer on page 159

Masyu

Draw a single continuous line around the grid that passes through all the circles. The line must enter and leave each box in the centre of one of its four sides.

Black Circle: Turn left or right in the box, and the line must pass straight through the next and previous boxes.

White Circle: Travel straight through the box, and the line must turn in the next and/or previous box.

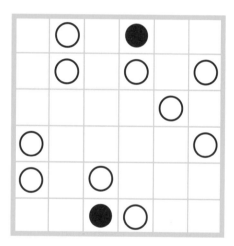

Answer on page 159

Matrix

Which of the boxed figures completes the set?

Answer on page 159

More or Less

The arrows indicate whether a number in a box is greater or smaller than an adjacent number. Complete the grid so that all rows and columns contain the numbers 1 to 5.

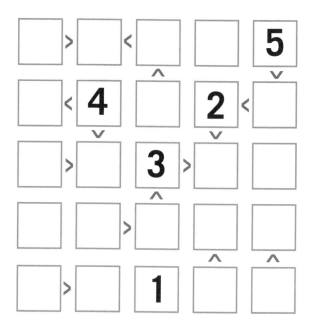

Answer on page 159

Paint by Numbers

Colour in the odd numbers to reveal... What?

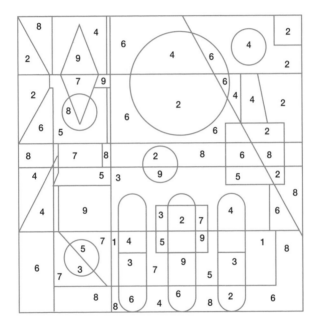

Answer on page 159

Face in the Crowd

Can you find one face in the crowd that isn't quite as happy as all the others?

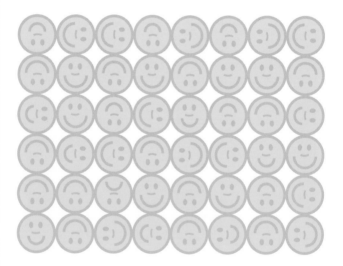

Answer on page 160

Piece Puzzle

Only one of these pieces fits the hole in our main picture – the others have all been altered slightly by our artist.
Can you place the missing pic?

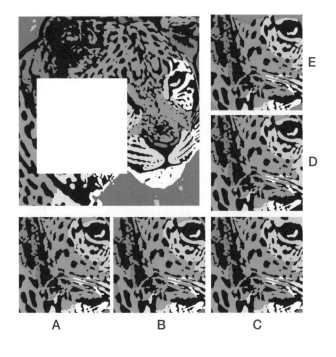

E

D

A

B

C

Answer on page 160

Scene It?

The four squares below can all be found in the picture grid, can you track them down? Beware, they may not be the right way up!

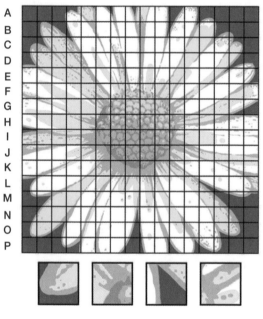

Answer on page 160

Spot the Difference

Can you spot ten differences between this pair of pictures?

Answer on page 160

Sudoku

Complete the grid so that all rows and columns, and each outlined block of nine squares, contain the numbers 1, 2, 3, 4, 5, 6, 7, 8 and 9.

8			1	7		2		
1		9			6		3	
	5			3	4		7	8
4			8	2		5	9	
	2		3		9		1	
	6							3
	4		7					2
		7		4	2	6	8	
	8		6		3		4	

Answer on page 160

Matrix

Which of the four boxed figures completes the set?

Answer on page 160

Riddle

An enclosure at the zoo contains both elephants and emus. If there are a total of 44 feet and 30 eyes, can you work out how many of each animal there is?

Answer on page 160

View From Above

Of the plan views below, only one of them is a true overhead representation of the scene shown here – can you work out which?

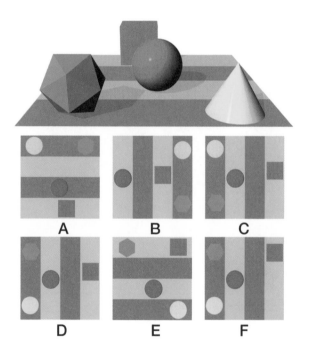

Answer on page 160

Bits and Pieces

Can you match the four broken tops of these vases with the bodies they belong to?

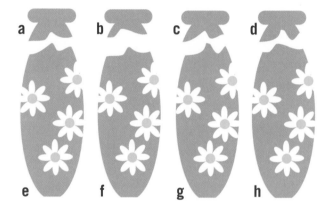

Answer on page 161

Cut and Fold

Which of the patterns below is created by this fold and cut?

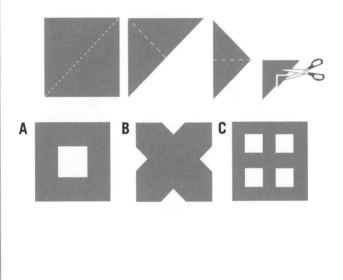

A **B** **C**

Answer on page 161

Location

Below is an altered view of a world famous landmark. Can you tell where it is?

Answer on page 161

Matrix

Which of the boxed figures completes the set?

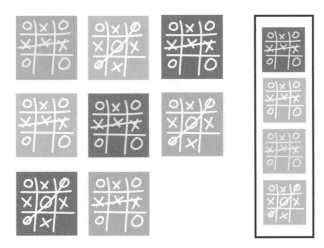

Answer on page 161

Mirror Image

Only one of these pictures is an exact mirror image of the first one. Can you spot it?

Answer on page 161

Number Jigsaw

The nine boxes that make up this grid can be rearranged to make a number. What number?

Answer on page 161

Patch of the Day

Place the shape in the grid so that no colour appears twice in the same row or column. Beware, the shape may not be the right way up!

Answer on page 161

Pipes

Which two of the four boxes below can successfully fix the gaps in the pipes?

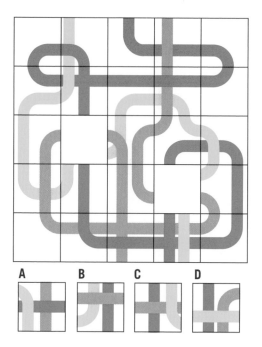

A B C D

Answer on page 161

Missing Link

What should replace the red square with the question mark so that the grid follows a pattern?

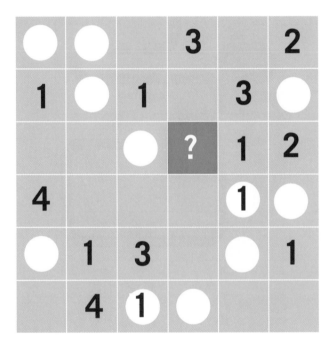

Answer on page 162

Picture Parts

Which box has exactly the right bits to make the pic?

Answer on page 162

Scene It?

The four squares below can all be found in the picture grid – can you track them down? Beware, they may not be the right way up!

Answer on page 162

Sum People

Work out what number is represented by which person and replace the question mark.

Symmetry

This picture, when finished, is symmetrical along a vertical line up the middle. Can you colour in the missing squares and work out what the picture is of?

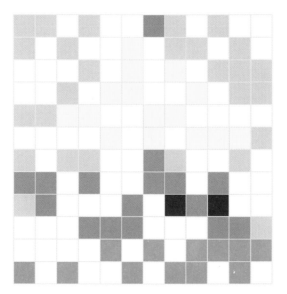

Answer on page 162

Usual Suspects

Officer Lassiter is having his new uniform and kit fitted. He has the helmet badge, but not the shoulder badges yet. He has his new radio, but hasn't yet received a new tie... Can you pick him out of the group?

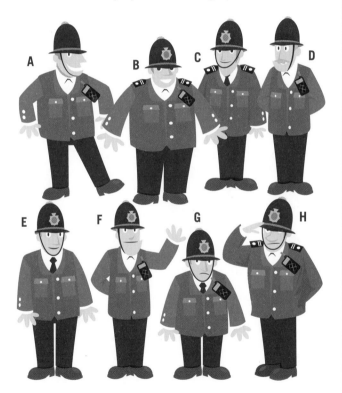

Answer on page 162

Where's the Pair?

Only two of these pictures are exactly the same. Can you spot the matching pair?

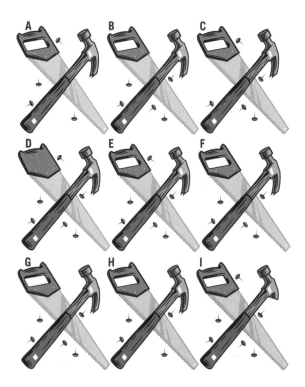

Answer on page 162

Which Wheel?

Which of the wheels, a, b, c, or d, is missing from the set below?

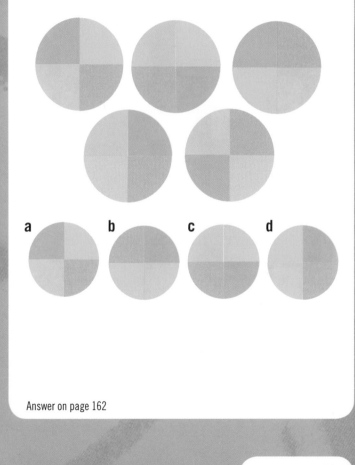

Answer on page 162

Odd Clocks

Madrid is 7 hours behind Tokyo, which is 1 hour behind Melbourne. It is 6.15 am on Saturday in Tokyo – What time is it in the other two cities?

TOKYO

MELBOURNE

MADRID

Answer on page 163

Where's the Pair?

Only two of the shapes below are exactly the same – can you find the matching pair?

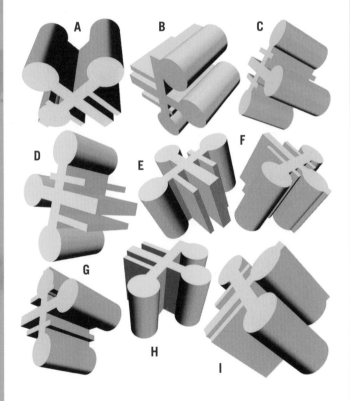

Answer on page 163

Where's the Pair

Only two of these pictures are exactly the same. Can you spot the matching pair?

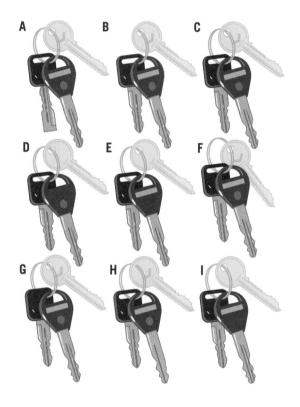

Answer on page 163

Usual Suspects

Banjo the clown has blue hair, but not a blue collar. He always wears a flower in his lapel and a comedy hat. Can you pick him out?

Answer on page 163

Sum Total

Replace the question marks with mathematical symbols (+, −, × or ÷) to make a working sum.

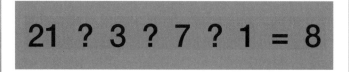

21 ? 3 ? 7 ? 1 = 8

Answer on page 163

Picture Parts

Which box has exactly the right bits to make the pic?

A   B   C

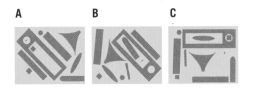

Answer on page 163

Magic Squares

Complete the square using nine consecutive numbers, so that all rows, columns and large diagonals add up to the same total.

8	**1**	**6**

Answer on page 163

Deep Sea Dresser

Arrange this set of diver pics in the correct order from boxers to ocean-prepared.

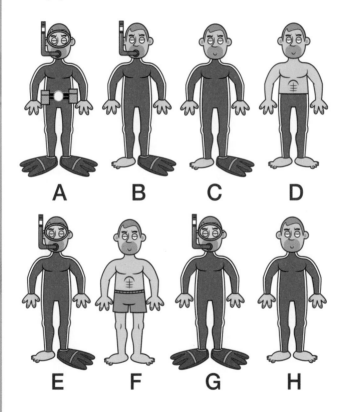

A   B   C   D

E   F   G   H

Answer on page 163

Can You Spot?

We've hidden ten spanners in this garage – Can you spot them all?

Answer on page 163

All Change

The colour of each triangle in pattern **B** is directly related to the colours in pattern **A**. Can you apply the same the rules and fill in pattern **C**?

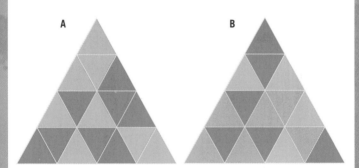

Answer on page 164

Game of Two Halves

Which two shapes below will pair up to create the top shape?

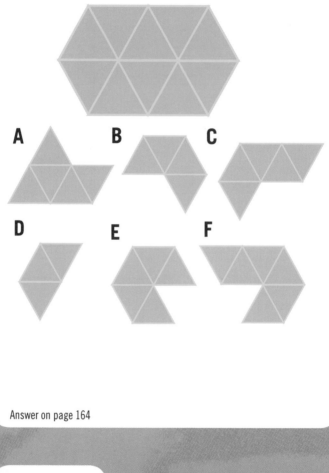

A

B

C

D

E

F

Answer on page 164

Hub Signs

What numbers should appear in the hubs of these number wheels?

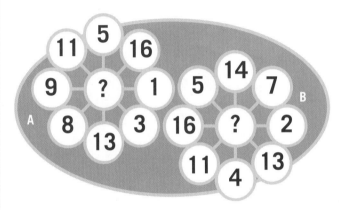

Answer on page 164

Riddle

Billy bought a bag of oranges on Monday and ate a third of them. On Tuesday he ate half of the oranges he had left. On Wednesday he found he had two oranges left. How many did he start with?

Answer on page 164

View From Above

Of the plan views below, only one of them is a true overhead representation of the scene shown here – can you work out which?

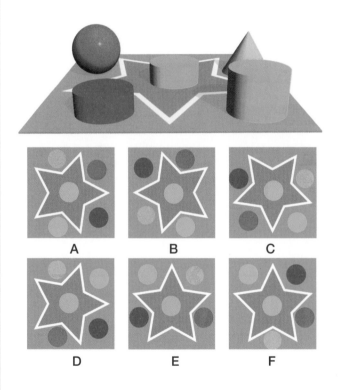

Answer on page 164

Cats and Cogs

Turn the handle in the indicated direction... Does the cat go up or down?

Answer on page 164

Checkers

Make a move for white so that eight black pieces are left, none of which are in the same column or row.

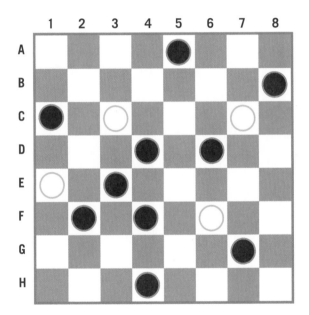

Answer on page 164

Get the Picture

These two grids, when merged together, will make a picture...
Of what?

Answer on page 165

In the Area

Can you work out the approximate area this bird is taking up?

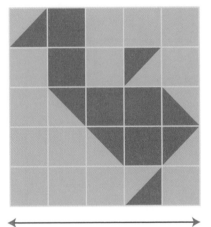

← 100 mm →

Answer on page 165

Matrix

Which of the boxed figures completes the set?

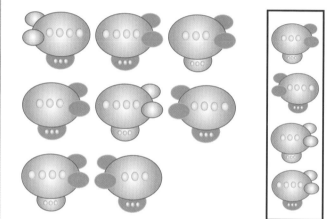

Answer on page 165

Missing Link

What should replace the square with the question mark so that the grid follows a pattern?

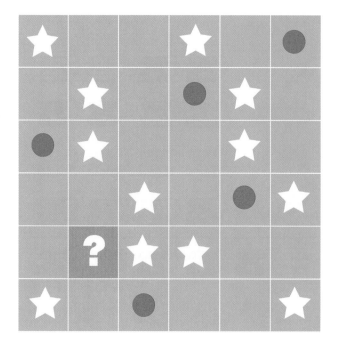

Answer on page 165

Symbol Sums

These symbols represent the numbers 1 to 4. If the green phone represents the number 3, can you work out what the other colour phones are representing and make a working sum?

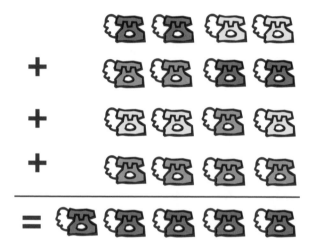

Answer on page 165

Symmetry

This picture, when finished, is symmetrical along a vertical line up the middle. Can you colour in the missing squares and work out what the picture is of?

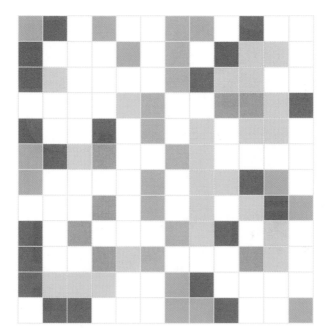

Answer on page 165

Where's the Pair?

Only two of these pictures are exactly the same. Can you spot the matching pair?

Answer on page 166

Sum Total

Replace the question marks with mathematical symbols (+, −, × or ÷) to make a working sum.

16 ? 2 ? 3 ? 1 = 6

Answer on page 166

Pool Puzzle

You're playing stripes in a game of pool, and you've cleaned up all your balls.
Just the black remains. Can you spot the shot?

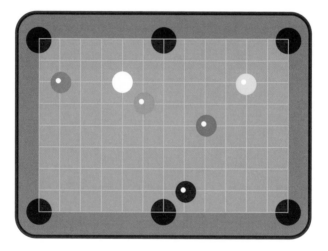

Answer on page 166

Piece Puzzle

Only one of these pieces fits the hole in our main picture – the others have all been altered slightly by our artist. Can you place the missing pic?

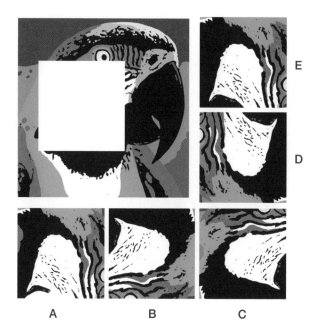

E

D

A

B

C

Answer on page 166

Patch of the Day

Place the shape over the grid so that no colour appears twice in the same row or column. Beware, the shape may not be the right way up!

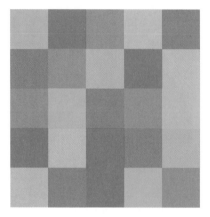

Answer on page 166

More or Less

The arrows indicate whether a number in a box is greater or smaller than an adjacent number. Complete the grid so that all rows and columns contain the numbers 1 to 5.

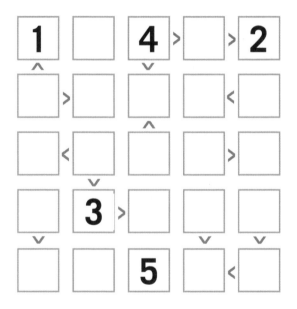

Answer on page 166

Riddle

It's night time in your bedroom and the light has broken. You're getting dressed and need a pair of socks. You've got 10 red, 8 white and 12 grey socks in a drawer – how many do you have to pull out in the dark before you know you have a matching pair?

Answer on page 166

All Change

The colour of each square in pattern B is directly related to the colours in pattern A. The square colours in pattern C relate to pattern B the same way. Can you apply the same the rules and fill in pattern D?

A

B

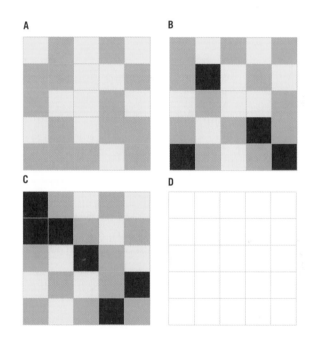

C

D

Answer on page 166

Boxes

Playing the game of boxes, each player takes it in turns to join two adjacent dots with a line. If a player's line completes a box, the player wins the box and has another go. It's your turn in the game below. To avoid giving your opponent a lot of boxes, what's your best move?

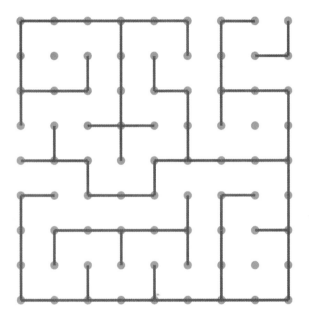

Answer on page 166

Double Drat

All these numbers appear twice in the box except one. Can you spot the singleton?

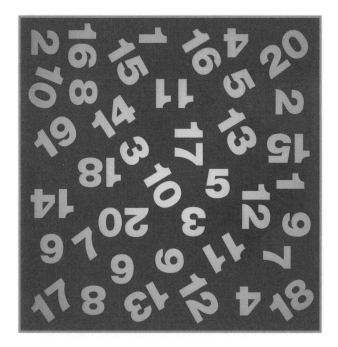

Answer on page 166

Boats and Buoys

Every buoy 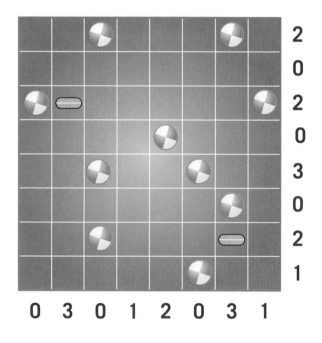 has one boat found horizontally or vertically adjacent to it. No boat can be in an adjacent square to another boat (even diagonally). The numbers by each row and column tell you how many boats are there. Can you locate all the boats?

2
0
2
0
3
0
2
1

0 3 0 1 2 0 3 1

Answer on page 167

86

Riddle

Tony and Tina go shopping and on the way home Tina says,
"Hey! If you gave me one of your bags, I'd have twice as many
as you – but if I gave you one of mine, we'd have the same number!
" Can you work out how many bags they have each?

Answer on page 167

Cubism

The shape below can be folded to make a cube. Which of the four cubes pictured below could it make?

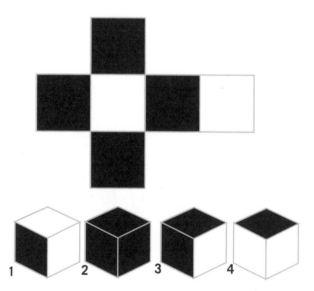

Answer on page 167

Cut and Fold

Which of the patterns below is created by this fold and cut?

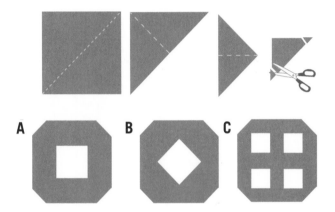

A

B

C

Answer on page 167

Latin Square

Complete the grid so that every row and column, and every outlined area, contains the letters A, B, C, D, E and F

Answer on page 167

Location

Below is an altered view of a world-famous landmark.
Can you tell where it is?

Answer on page 167

Masyu

Draw a single continuous line around the grid that passes through all the circles. The line must enter and leave each box in the centre of one of its four sides.

Black Circle: Turn left or right in the box, and the line must pass straight through the next and previous boxes.

White Circle: Travel straight through the box, and the line must turn in the next and/or previous box.

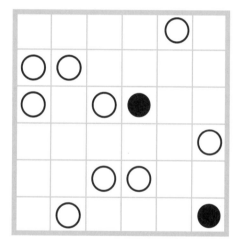

Answer on page 167

Matrix

Which of the boxed figures completes the set?

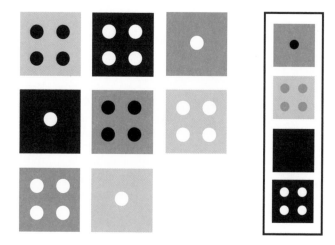

Answer on page 167

Next!

Which of the balls, A, B, C or D is the logical next step in this sequence?

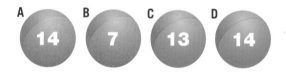

Answer on page 168

Next!

Which of the balls, A, B, C or D is the logical next step in this sequence?

Answer on page 168

Riddle

A fish is 45 centimetres long, and its head is as long as its tail. If its head were twice as long as it really is, the head and tail together would be as long as the middle part of the fish. How long is each part of the fish?

Answer on page 168

Bits and Pieces

Can you match the four broken windows with the pieces of glass below?

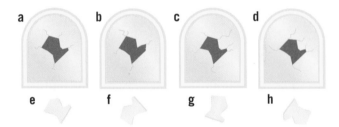

Answer on page 168

Block Party

Assuming all blocks that are not visible from this angle are present, how many blocks have been removed from this 6 × 6 × 6 cube?

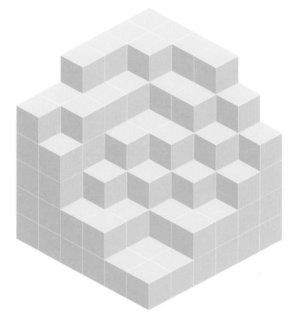

Answer on page 168

Picture Parts

Which box has exactly the right bits to make the pic?

Answer on page 168

Pots of Dots

How many dots should there be in the hole in this pattern?

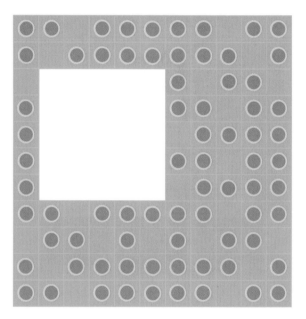

Answer on page 168

Get the Picture

These two grids, when merged together, will make a picture...
Of what?

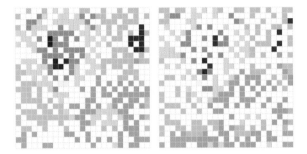

Answer on page 168

Rainbow Reckoning

This wall is to be painted in Green, Blue and Lilac, with no adjacent bricks to be in the same colour. Can you work out what colour the window frame should be?

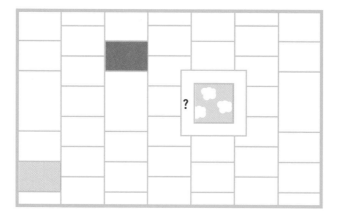

Answer on page 169

Sum Total

Replace the question marks with mathematical symbols (+, −, × or ÷) to make a working sum.

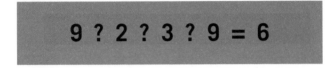

9 ? 2 ? 3 ? 9 = 6

Answer on page 169

Spot the Difference

Can you Spot ten differences between this pair of pictures?

Answer on page 169

Symmetry

This picture, when finished, is symmetrical along a vertical line up the middle. Can you colour in the missing squares and work out what the picture is of?

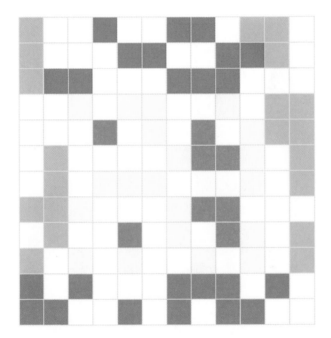

Answer on page 169

Scene It?

The four squares below can all be found in the picture grid – can you track them down? Beware, they may not be the right way up!

Answer on page 169

Riddle

You are in a room, blindfolded, with a bowl containing 50, 20, 10 and 5 dollar bills. You are allowed to take notes out of the bowl one at a time until you have four notes of the same value. What's the largest amount of cash you could end up with?

Answer on page 169

Block Party

Assuming all blocks that are not visible from this angle are present, how many blocks have been removed from this 5 × 5 × 5 cube?

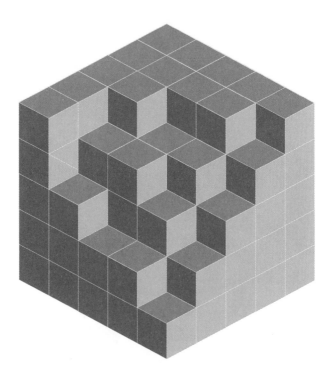

Answer on page 169

Boxes

In the game of boxes, each player takes it in turns to join two adjacent dots with a line. If a player's line completes a box, the player wins the box and has another go. It's your turn in the game below. Can you give your opponent just one box?

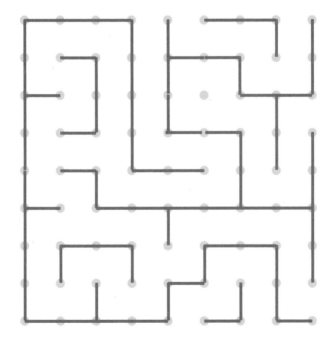

Answer on page 169

Boxes

In the game of boxes, each player takes it in turns to join two adjacent dots with a line. If a player's line completes a box, the player wins the box and has another go. It's your turn in the game below. Can you give your opponent just one box?

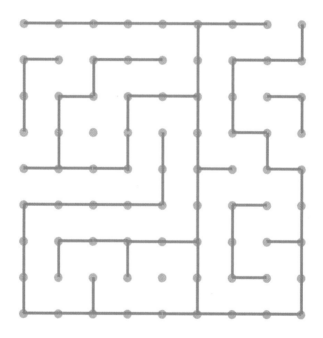

Answer on page 170

Checkers

Make a move for white so that eight black pieces are left, none of which are in the same column or row.

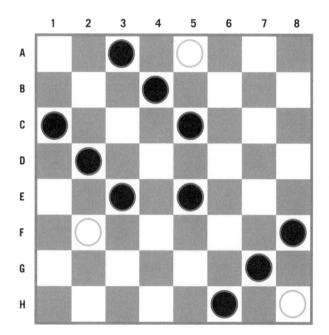

Answer on page 170

Double Drat

All these letters appear twice in the box except one. Can you spot the singleton?

Answer on page 170

Dressing Snowman

Arrange this set of snowman pics in the correct order from bare ball of snow to fully fledged.

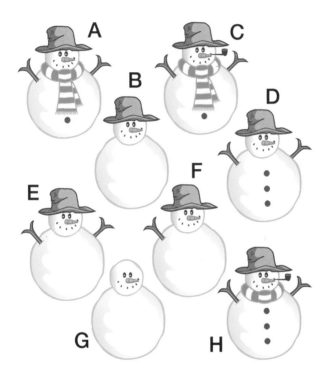

Answer on page 170

Game of Two Halves

Which two shapes below will pair up to create the top shape?

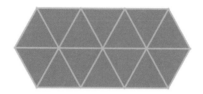

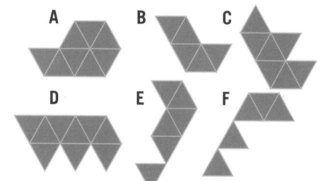

A

B

C

D

E

F

Answer on page 170

Get the Picture

These two grids, when merged together, will make a picture...
Of what?

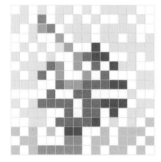 

Answer on page 170

Gridlock

Which square correctly completes the grid?

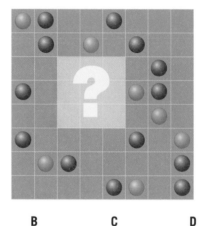

A **B** **C** **D**

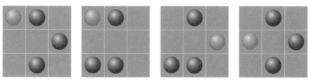

Answer on page 170

Riddle

Celebrity chef, Gordon Ramsfoot discovered one Sunday morning that his toaster had broken and he had three hungry kids on his hands. It takes exactly one minute to toast one side of a piece of bread using the grill, but the grill only takes two pieces of bread at a time. In a terrible hurry as always, can you work out how he managed to make three pieces of toast, using the grill, in just three minutes?

Answer on page 170

X and O

The numbers around the edge of the grid describe the number of X's in the vertical, horizontal and diagonal lines connecting with that square. Complete the grid so that there is an X or O in every square.

1	2	4	4	3	2
6					4
3					4
2		X			3
2			X		1
2	3	2	2	5	1

Answer on page 171

Gridlock

One of the squares below correctly replaces the question mark and completes the grid. Can you work out which?

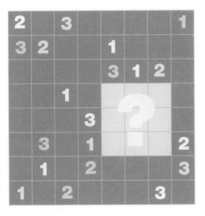

A   B   C   D

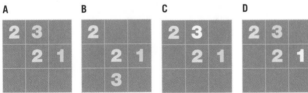

Answer on page 171

Where's the Pair?

Only two of these pictures are exactly the same. Can you spot the matching pair?

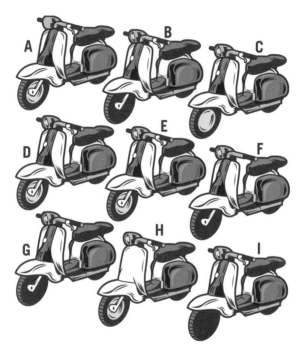

Answer on page 171

Hue Goes There

Three of the sections below can be found in our main grid, one cannot. Can you spot the section that doesn't belong? Beware, the sections might not be the same way round!

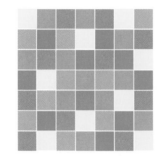

a b c d

Answer on page 171

Usual Suspects

Flutter the fairy has a magic wand and wings, but she doesn't wear a crown and hasn't got a bow on her dress. Can you pick her out?

Answer on page 171

In the Area

Can you work out the approximate area this letter Q is taking up?

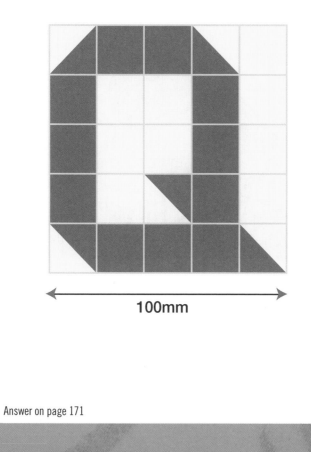

100mm

Answer on page 171

Think of a number

Officers Kaplutski and Wojowitz like a doughnut while they work. On a week long stakeout, Kaplutski ate 12 jam doughnuts and Wojowitz ate 28. What percentage of all the doughnuts eaten did Wojowitz account for?

Answer on page 171

Jigsaw

Which three of the pieces below can complete the jigsaw?

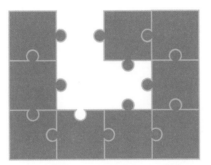

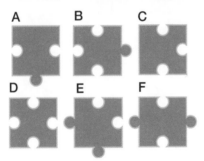

A　B　C

D　E　F

Answer on page 171

Symmetry

This picture, when finished, is symmetrical along a vertical line up the middle. Can you colour in the missing squares and work out what the picture is of?

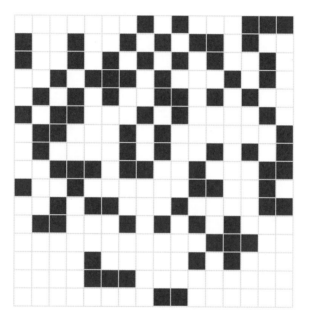

Answer on page 171

Logic Sequence

The dice below have been rearranged. Can you work out the new sequence from the clues given below?

The blue dice is between two odd numbers. The green dice is immediately to the left of the number 1. The number 2 is immediately to the right of the yellow dice. The two dice on the far left hand side add up to ten.

Answer on page 171

Matrix

Which of the boxed figures completes the set?

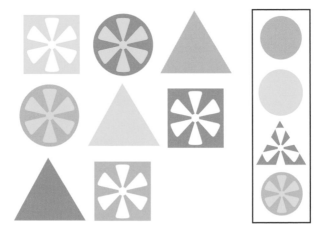

Answer on page 172

Matrix

Which of the boxed figures completes the set?

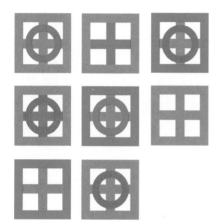 

Answer on page 172

Matrix

Which of the boxed figures completes the set?

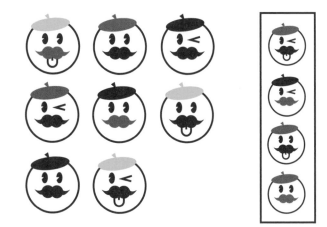

Answer on page 172

Mirror Image

Only one of these pictures is an exact mirror image of the first one. Can you spot it?

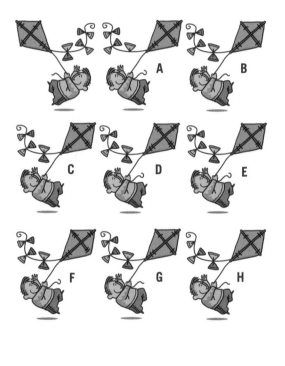

Answer on page 173

Missing Link

What should replace the square with the question mark so that the grid follows a pattern?

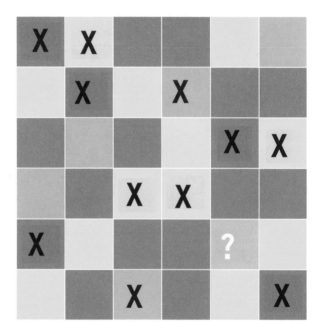

Answer on page 173

Next!

Which of the balls, A, B, C or D is the logical next step in his sequence?

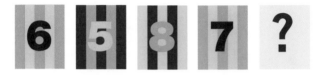

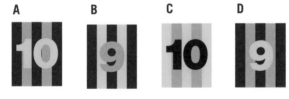

Answer on page 173

Number Mountain

Replace the question marks with numbers so that each pair of blocks adds up to the block directly above them.

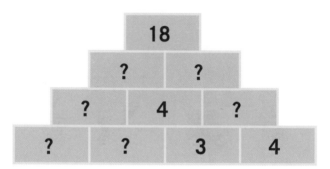

Answer on page 173

Odd Clocks

Paris is 2 hours behind Athens, which is 2 hours behind Karachi.
It is 1.50 am on Sunday in Athens – what time is it in the other two cities?

ATHENS

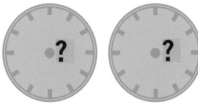

KARACHI   **PARIS**

Answer on page 173

Paint by Numbers

Colour in the odd numbers to reveal... What?

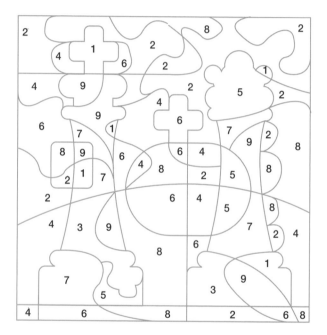

Answer on page 173

Picture Parts

Which box contains exactly the right bits to make the pic?

Answer on page 173

Picture Parts

Which box contains exactly the right bits to make the pic?

A   B   C

Answer on page 173

Piece Puzzle

Only one of these pieces fits the hole in our main picture - the others have all been altered slightly by our artist. Can you place the missing pic?

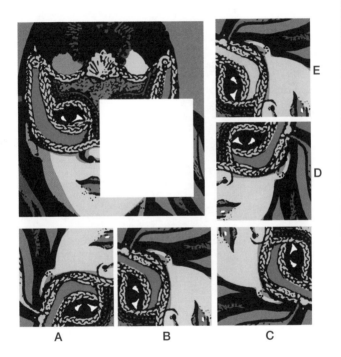

A B C

Answer on page 173

Pots of Dots

How many dots should there be in the hole in this pattern?

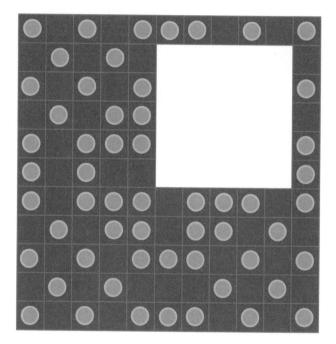

Answer on page 174

Rainbow Reckoning

This wall is to be painted in Green, Blue and Lilac, with no adjacent bricks to be in the same colour. Can you work out what colour the bottom right hand corner should be?

Answer on page 174

Reach for the Stars

Can you find three perfect five-pointed stars in this colourful collection?

Answer on page 174

Sum Total

Replace the question marks with mathematical symbols (+, −, × or ÷) to make a working sum.

4 ? 8 ? 7 ? 5 = 5

Answer on page 174

Scales

The arms of these scales are divided into sections – a weight two sections away from the middle will be twice as heavy as a weight one section away. Can you arrange the supplied weights in such a way as to balance the whole scale?

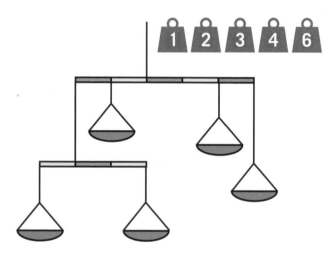

Answer on page 174

Sum People

Work out what number is represented by which person and replace the question mark.

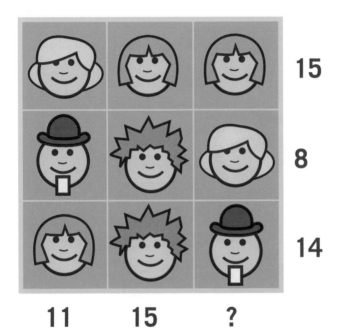

15

8

14

11   15   ?

Answer on page 174

Scene It?

The four squares below can all be found in the picture grid – can you track them down? Beware, they may not be the right way up!

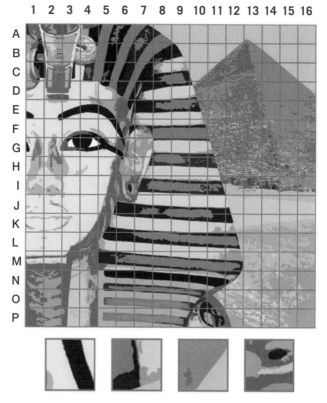

Answer on page 174

Sudoku Sixpack

Complete the grid so that every row, column and long diagonal contains the numbers 1, 2, 3, 4, 5 and 6

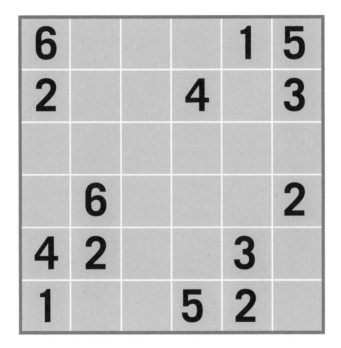

Answer on page 174

Shape Shifting

Fill in the empty squares so that each row, column and long diagonal contains five different symbols.

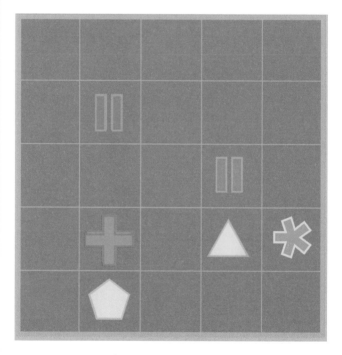

Answer on page 174

Spot the Difference

Can you spot ten differences between this pair of pictures?

Answer on page 175

Shape Stacker

Can you work out the logic behind the numbers in these shapes, and suggest a number to replace the question mark?

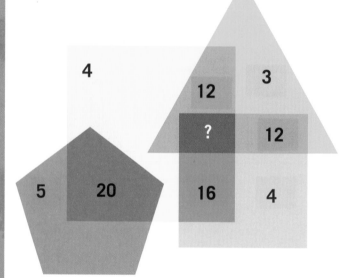

Answer on page 175

Shuffle

Fill in the grid so that each row, column and long diagonal contains four different shapes and the letters A, B, C and D.

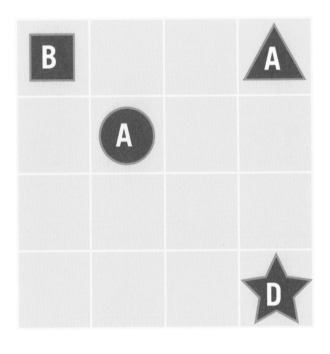

Answer on page 175

Shuffle

Fill in the shuffle box so that each row, column and long diagonal contains four different shapes and the letters A, B, C and D

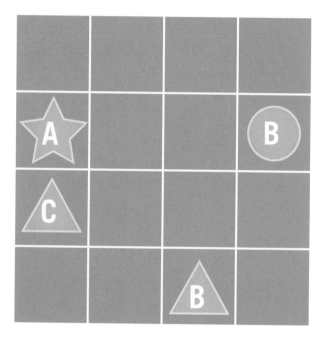

Answer on page 175

Signpost

Can you crack the logical secret behind the distances to these great cities, and work out how far it is to Karachi?

NEW YORK 11

OSLO 2

KARACHI ?

PARIS 5

GDANSK 13

Answer on page 175

Sum Total

Replace the question marks with mathematical symbols (+, −, × or ÷) to make a working sum.

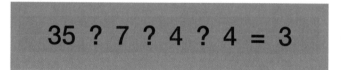

35 ? 7 ? 4 ? 4 = 3

Answer on page 175

Riddle

In my shed at home I have some hamsters and some hamster cages. If I put one hamster in each cage I'd have one hamster too many. But if I put two hamsters in each cage, I'd have one cage left over... How many hamsters and cages have I got?

Answer on page 175

Piece Puzzle

Only one of these pieces fits the hole in our main picture – the others have all been altered slightly by our artist. Can you place the missing pic?

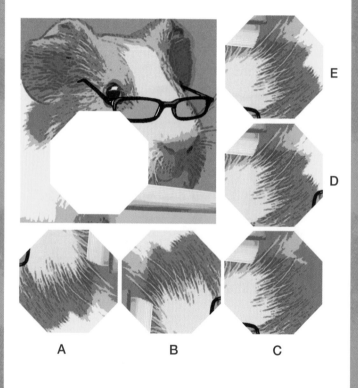

Answer on page 175

Answers

Page 6
Answer: A and G, B and D,
C and H, E and F

Page 7
Solution: A line on the right or bottom
of this square will only give up one
box to your opponent

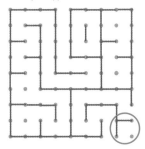

Page 8

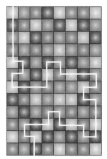

Page 9
Answer: A

Page 10

Page 11
Solution: C and D

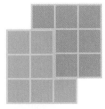

Page 12
Solution below

Page 13
Answer: A. Each row and line in the grid
contains three green, three red and two
yellow squares

Answers

Page 14
Answer: 5,000 square millimetres. Each 20 x 20 square represents 400 mm². 12 and a half squares are used

Page 15
Answer: A, C and E

Page 16
Answer: A and G are the pair

Page 17

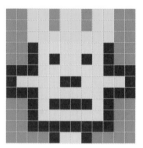

Page 18
Answer 6

1
2
3
4

Page 19

Page 20

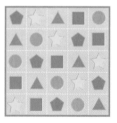

Page 21
Answer: F 4, D 14, L 2, L 15

Answers

Page 22
Answer: Yellow

Page 23
Answer: 13

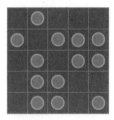

Page 24
Answer: A

Page 25
Answer: 1.55 am on Wednesday in Singapore and 2.55 pm on Tuesday in Buenos Aires

Page 26

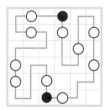

Page 27

Answer:

 Each horizontal and vertical line contains a white star, a yellow star and a circled star. Each line contains a green and orange halved circle that has been turned through 0 degrees, 90 degrees and 180 degrees. The missing image should contain a white star, and a circle that has been turned through 90 degrees

Page 28

3 >	1 <	2	4	5
1 <	4	5	2 <	3
5 >	2	3 >	1	4
2	5 >	4	3	1
4 >	3	1	5	2

Page 29
Answer: A Church

Answers

Page 30
Answer: The 5th face down in the third column

Page 31
Answer: A

Page 32
Answer: B2, G6, M2, G11

Page 33

Page 34

8	3	4	1	7	5	2	6	9
1	7	9	2	8	6	4	3	5
2	5	6	9	3	4	1	7	8
4	1	3	8	2	7	5	9	6
7	2	5	3	6	9	8	1	4
9	6	8	4	5	1	7	2	3
6	4	1	7	9	8	3	5	2
3	9	7	5	4	2	6	8	1
5	8	2	6	1	3	9	4	7

Page 35
Answer:

Each vertical and horizontal line contains one shape with all green triangles, one with all pink triangles and one with half pink and half green triangles. Each line also contains two shapes with a white dot in the centre and one with no white dot. The missing shape must have all green triangles and a white dot

Page 36
Answer: 7 elephants and 8 emus

Page 37
Answer: D

Answers

Page 38
Answer: A and F, B and H,
C and E, D and G

Page 39
Answer: C

Page 40
Answer: The Leaning Tower of Pisa

Page 41
Answer: Each horizontal amd vertical
line contains two games where X's
win, and one where O's win. Each line
contains a green, an orange and a
blue square. Each line contains two
white games and a yellow game. The
missing picture should be of a yellow
game on a green square where X's win

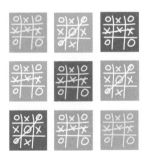

Page 42
Answer: D

Page 43

Page 44

Page 45
Answer: A and B

Answers

Page 46
Answer: A blue square containing a white circle and a black number 2. Each row and column contains two white circles and numbers that add up to five

Page 47
Answer: A

Page 48
Answer: M13, J16, A13, N7

Page 49
Answer: 10

1

2

3

5

Page 50

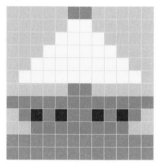

Page 51
Answer: Officer Lassiter is policeman F

Page 52
Answer: F and G are the pair

Page 53
Answer: b

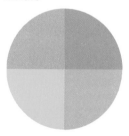

Answers

Page 54
Answer: 7.15 am on Saturday in Melbourne
11.15 pm on Friday in Madrid

Page 55
Answer: D and E are the pair

Page 56
Answer: E and I are the pair

Page 57
Answer: Banjo is clown C

Page 58
Answer: $21 \times 3 \div 7 - 1 = 8$

Page 59
Answer: C

Page 60

Answer

Page 61
Answer: F, D, H, C, B, E, G, A

Page 62

Answers

Page 63

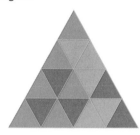

Answer: If its bordering triangles are predominantly orange, a triangle becomes red. If they are predominantly red, it becomes orange. If the bordering cells are equal in number, the triangle becomes pink, and if the bordering triangles have now become predominantly pink, it also becomes pink

Page 64
Answer: B and F

Page 65
Answer:
A) 8 – subtract the numbers opposite each other
B) 18 – Add the opposite numbers

Page 66
Answer: Six. He ate two on Monday and two more on Tuesday

Page 67
Answer: D

Page 68
Answer: Down

Page 69

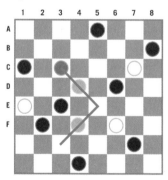

Answers

Page 70

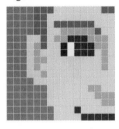

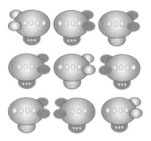

Page 71

Answer: 3400 square millimetres. Each 20 x 20 square represents 400 mm². 5 squares (2000 mm²) and 7 half-square triangles (1400 mm²) form the bird

Page 72

Answer: Each horizontal and vertical line contains two airships with green fins, and one with silvery fins. Each line contains two airships with green gondolas underneath, and one with a silvery gondola. Each line contains two airships facing left and one facing right. Each line contains two airships with four lights on the balloon, and one with three lights. The missing image has silvery fins, a green gondola, faces left and has four lights on the balloon

Page 73

Answer: A green square containing a red dot. All the rows and columns should contain two white stars and one red dot

Page 74

Answer:
red 1	blue 2
green 3	yellow 4

Page 75

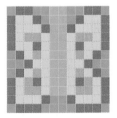

Answers

Page 76
Answer: F and H are the pair

Page 77
Answer: $16 + 2 \div 3 \times 1 = 6$

Page 78

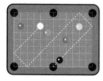

Page 79
Answer: B

Page 80

Page 81

Page 82
Answer: Just 4

Page 83

Solution: If its bordering squares (not diagonals) are predominantly green, a square becomes green. If they are predominantly yellow, it becomes yellow. If the bordering cells are equal In number, the square becomes black, and if the bordering squares have now become predominantly black, it also becomes black

Page 84
Answer: A line on the top or bottom of this square will only give up one box to your opponent

Page 85
Answer: 19

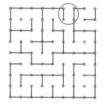

Answers

Page 86

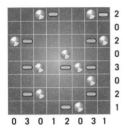

0 3 0 1 2 0 3 1

Page 87

Answer: Tony has 5 bags, Tina has 7

Page 88

Answer: 3

Page 89

Answer: B

Page 90

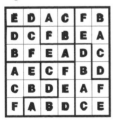

Page 91

Answer: The Statue of Liberty

Page 92

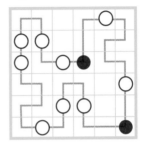

Page 93

Answer: Each horizontal or vertical line contains a group of 4 black dots, a group of 4 white dots and a single white dot. Each line contains a light blue symbol, a dark blue symbol and a black symbol. The missing picture must be a black symbol with 4 black (and therefore invisible) dots

Answers

Page 94
Answer: D. The colours on the ball are alternating, while the number on it is increasing, by 1, then 2, then 3 etc

Page 95
Answer: D. The star and circle are swapping places each time. The smallest shape is taking the colour of the previous background square. The background square is taking the colour of the previous medium-sized shape, and the medium-sized shape is taking the colour of the previous smallest shape

Page 96
Answer: The head and tail are 9 centimetres long, the middle is 27 centimetres long

Page 97
Answer: A and G, B and H, C and F, D and E

Page 98
Answer: 76

Page 99
Answer: C

Page 100
Answer: 18

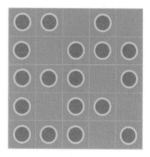

Page 101

Answers

Page 102
Answer: Lilac

Page 103
Answer: $9 \times 2 \times 3 \div 9 = 6$

Page 104

Page 105
Answer: M14, M2, F9, A4

Page 106

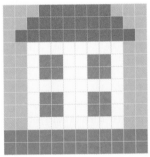

Page 107
Answer: $305 dollars. Three of each denomination and one more $50 bill

Page 108
Answer: 24

Page 109
Answer: A line on either side of this square will only give up one box to your opponent

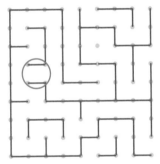

Answers

Page 110
Solution: A line on either side of this square will only give up one box to your opponent

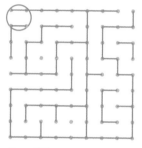

Page 111

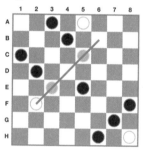

Page 112
Answer: A

Page 113
Answer: G, B, F, E, D, H, A, C

Page 114
Answer: D and F

Page 115

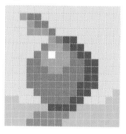

Page 116
Answer: B. Each row and line in the grid should contain two blue balls and one red ball

Page 117
Answer: Bread A and B go under the grill. One minute later, Gordon tuns bread A over and swaps bread B for Bread C. One minute later he removes bread A, turns over bread C and puts B back under for a further minute

Answers

Page 118

1	2	4	4	3	2
6	**X**	**O**	**X**	**X**	4
3	**X**	**O**	**O**	**X**	4
2	**O**	**X**	**O**	**O**	3
2	**O**	**O**	**X**	**O**	1
2	3	2	2	5	1

Page 119

Answer: A. Each row and column in the grid should contain the numbers 1, 2 and 3, and one each of numbers coloured yellow, blue and pink

Page 120

Answer: B and G are the pair

Page 121

Answer: b is the odd shape out

Page 122

Answer: Flutter is fairy D

Page 123

Answer: 5400 square millimetres. Each 20×20 square represents $400mm^2$. 11 squares ($4400mm^2$) and 5 half-square triangles ($1000mm^2$) form the Q

Page 124

Answer: 70 percent. Total number of doughnuts - 40, becomes 100 when multiplied by 2.5. Multiply the other numbers by 2.5 to get percentages

Page 125

Answer: B, C and F

Page 126

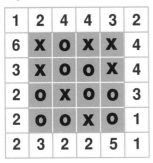

Page 127

Answers

Page 128

Answer: Each horizontal and vertical line contains 1 circle, 1 square and 1 triangle. Each line contains a yellow star, a white star and one picture without a star. Each line contains an orange symbol, a red symbol and a yellow symbol. The missing picture must be a yellow circle containing a yellow star

Page 129

Answer: Each horizontal and vertical line contains two green

frames and a pink frame. Each horizontal and vertical line contains two green crosses and a pink cross. Each line contains a purple circle, a pink circle and no circle. The missing picture must be a green frame, with a pink cross and a pink circle

Page 130

Answer: Each horizontal and vertical line contains two black moustaches and a brown moustache. Each line contains one wink, and one tongue. Each line contains a yellow hat, a brown hat and a black hat. The missing picture must have a brown moustache, no wink, no tongue and a brown hat

Answers

Page 131
Answer: B

Page 132
Answer: A blue square containing a cross. All the rows and columns should contain two crosses, three brown squares, two yellow squares and one blue square

Page 133
Answer: A. The numbers are following a pattern of minus 1, plus 3. The number is taking the colour of the old inside stripes, the inside stripes are taking the colour of the old outside stripes and the outside stripes are taking the colour of the old number

Page 134

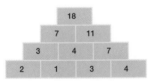

Page 135
Answer: 3.50am on Sunday in Karachi, 11.50pm on Saturday in Paris

Page 136

Page 137
Answer: B

Page 138
Answer: A

Page 139
Answer: B

Answers

Page 140
Answer: 12

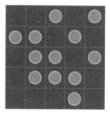

Page 141
Answer: Green

Page 142

Page 143
Answer: $4 \times 8 - 7 \div 5 = 5$

Page 144

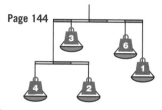

Page 145
Answer: 11

1

3

4

7

Page 146
Answer: E3, C9, D16, I6

Page 147

6	4	3	2	1	5
2	5	1	4	6	3
5	1	2	3	4	6
3	6	4	1	5	2
4	2	5	6	3	1
1	3	6	5	2	4

Page 148

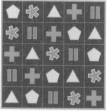

Answers

Page 149

Page 150

Answer: 48.

The numbers represent the number of sides in the shape they occupy. When shapes overlap, the numbers are multiplied. $3 \times 4 \times 4 = 48$

Page 151

Page 152

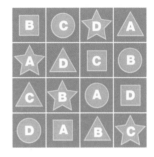

Page 153

Answer: 6. Score three for each consonant and two for a vowel. Subtract the vowel total from the consonant total. $12 - 6 = 6$

Page 154

Answer: $35 - 7 \div 4 - 4 = 3$

Page 155

Answer: 4 hamsters and 3 cages

Page 156

Answer: E

Your Puzzle Notes